The Six
Healing Sounds

The Six Healing Sounds

Taoist Techniques for Balancing Chi

Mantak Chia

Destiny Books
Rochester, Vermont

Destiny Books
One Park Street
Rochester, Vermont 05767
www.DestinyBooks.com

Destiny Books is a division of Inner Traditions International

Originally published in Thailand in 2006 by Universal Tao Publications under the
title *Cosmic Healing Sounds: Sounds That Heal*

Library of Congress Cataloging-in-Publication Data
Chia, Mantak, 1944–
  [Cosmic healing sounds]
  The six healing sounds : Taoist techniques for balancing chi / Mantak Chia.
      p. cm.
  Originally published: Cosmic healing sounds : sounds that heal. Thailand : Univer-
sal Tao Publications, 2006.
  Includes index.
  Summary: "The Six Healing Sounds that keep the vital organs in optimal
condition"—Provided by publisher.
  ISBN 978-1-59477-156-9 (pbk.)
  1. Taoism. 2. Hygiene, Taoist. I. Title. II. Title: Taoist techniques for balancing
chi.
  BL1920.C25755 2009
  615.8'51—dc22
                                                                    2008030970
Printed and bound in India by Replika Press Pvt. Ltd.

10   9

Text design and layout by Priscilla Baker
This book was typeset in Janson, with Present and Futura used as display typefaces

Contents

Acknowledgments

We extend our gratitude to the many generations of Taoist masters who have passed on their special lineage, in the form of an unbroken oral transmission, over thousands of years. We wish to especially thank Taoist Master Yi Eng for his patience and openness in transmitting the formulas of Taoist Inner Alchemy. We also wish to thank the thousands of unknown men and women of the Chinese healing arts who developed many of the methods and ideas presented in this book.

We offer our eternal gratitude to our parents and teachers for their many gifts to us. Remembering them brings joy and satisfaction to our continued efforts in presenting the Universal Tao System. As always, their contribution has been crucial in presenting the concepts and techniques of the Universal Tao.

We thank the many contributors essential to this book's final form: The editorial and production staff at Inner Traditions/Destiny Books for their efforts to clarify the text and produce a handsome new edition of the book, Nancy Yeilding for her line edit of the new edition, and the artist, Juan Li, for the use of his beautiful and visionary paintings and drawings, illustrating Taoist esoteric practices.

We wish to thank the following people for their assistance in producing the original edition of this book: Dena Saxer for her writing and editorial contributions; Udon for his illustrations, book layout, and beautiful cover; Wilbert Wils and Jean Chilton for their assistance in preparing, editing, and proofreading the manuscript; and Jettaya Phaobtong and Saumya Comer for their editorial contributions to the revised edition.

A special thank-you goes to our Thai Production Team: Raruen Keawpadung, computer graphics; Saysunee Yongyod, photographer; Udon Jandee, illustrator; and Saniem Chaisarn, production designer.

Putting the Six Healing Sounds into Practice

The practices described in this book have been used successfully for thousands of years by Taoists trained by personal instruction. Readers should not undertake them without receiving personal transmission and training from a certified instructor of the Universal Tao, since certain of these practices, if done improperly, may cause injury or result in health problems. This book is intended to supplement individual training by the Universal Tao and to serve as a reference guide for these practices. Anyone who undertakes these practices on the basis of this book alone, does so entirely at his or her own risk.

The meditations, practices, and techniques described herein are not intended to be used as an alternative or substitute for professional medical treatment and care. If any readers are suffering from illnesses based on mental or emotional disorders, an appropriate professional health care practitioner or therapist should be consulted. Such problems should be corrected before you start training.

This book does not attempt to give any medical diagnosis, treatment, prescription, or remedial recommendation in relation to any human disease, ailment, suffering, or physical condition whatsoever.

The Universal Tao and its staff and instructors cannot be responsible for the consequences of any practice or misuse of the information contained in this book. If the reader undertakes any exercise without strictly following the instructions, notes, and warnings, the responsibility must lie solely with the reader.

What Is the Universal Tao?

The Universal Tao is a self-help system for curing and preventing illness and stress, and for enhancing all aspects of life. Its key concept is increasing vital energy, or chi, through easy techniques and physical exercises. This life-force energy is then circulated through the acupuncture meridians of the body and channeled into health, vitality, balanced emotions, and creative and spiritual expression.

A practical system accessible to everybody, the Universal Tao is a modern expression of centuries-old Taoist practices. Many of these techniques were formerly known only to an elite group of Taoist masters and handpicked students. After formulating these powerful practices into a comprehensive system, I began teaching them to the public at large in my native Thailand in 1973. In 1978 I brought this system to the Western world. I then opened the Universal Tao Center in New York and began teaching the practices there. Today we teach our system in various places throughout the United States and Europe, as well as in Thailand. Though spiritual in its foundation, the Universal Tao is not a religion. It is compatible with all religions, as well as with agnosticism and atheism. There are no rituals to perform and no gurus to surrender to: the master and the teacher are highly respected, but are not deified.

The Universal Tao system has three levels:

Level I concentrates on universal energy, strengthening and calming the body

Level II concentrates on changing negative emotions into strong, positive energy

Level III concentrates on creative and spiritual practices

All levels include both mental (meditative) practices and physical disciplines, such as Tai Chi, Papua, and Iron Shirt Chi Kung.

This book covers the Six Healing Sounds, one of the beginning practices of Level I. Level I also includes the Microcosmic Orbit, which is covered in my book, *Healing Light of the Tao,* and the Inner Smile, which should be used to begin every meditation in the Healing Tao system. For instructions on this technique, see *The Inner Smile: Increasing Chi through the Cultivation of Joy.* For the most profound results, you should make all three of these practices of Level I an integral part of your life. For a description of other courses and for the addresses and phone numbers of the Universal Tao centers, see the end of this book.

TAOISM AND SOME BASIC CONCEPTS IN CHINESE HEALING

Taoism is the five- to eight-thousand-year-old foundation of Chinese philosophy and medicine. It is also the mother of acupuncture and the inspiration for modern body-oriented therapies, such as acupressure, Rolfing, and the Feldenkrais method. The Tao has been described as "natural law" or "natural order," "the constantly changing cycle of the seasons," "an art," "a method," "a power," and "a path of direction."

In the Taoist view, harmony and balance are essential for health. The body is seen as a whole; therefore, stress or injury to one organ, gland, or system weakens the entire body. The body is also self-regulating and will naturally move toward balance if allowed.

The Taoist system links each organ to one of the five elements in nature: metal, water, wood, fire, or earth. It also connects each organ to a season of the year (the season in which the organ is dominant or working the hardest), a color, and a quality in nature (such as wet, dry, or windy). These relationships often describe the characteristics of the given organ. For example, the heart is linked to summer, fire, and red; a healthy heart is associated with excitement and warmth.

According to Taoism, the body, mind, and spirit are totally integrated. Therefore, Chinese medicine finds that negative emotions, such as anger, fear, or cruelty, and excessive amounts of positive emotions, such as too much joy or excitement, can injure the organs and cause disease. By helping to balance the emotions, the Six Healing Sounds help to improve health.

ILLNESS STARTS AS AN ENERGY-LEVEL PROBLEM

Illness is caused by a blockage of energy. Too much or too little energy in one part of the body results in disease to that part and stresses the entire body. The Universal Tao teaches us how to correct this imbalance by awakening the chi, or vital energy, and circulating it to the needed areas.

A problem may exist for many years before it physically manifests itself as a disease. It may appear as a blockage or decrease of energy level, which then leads to a chi imbalance in particular parts or organs of the body. If we become aware of the energy imbalance when it first occurs, we have a long grace period in which to correct it.

Many people don't regard bad temper or negative emotions as sickness. In Taoism we regard these as the beginning of the imbalance of the chi energy in the system, just like bad breath or body odor can be the beginning signs of weakness or illness of the liver, kidneys, or stomach. Stubbornness can be caused by an imbalance of heart energy. Malodorous sweat can be due to a dysfunction of the kidneys, which have lost the filtering function to eliminate excess water contained in the body fluids. Cowardice and fear can be due to an imbalance of the lung or kidney energy. Back pain can be caused by an imbalance of the kidneys and bladder, and many other bad behaviors and physical ailments can be traced to an imbalance of the chi energy in different parts of the body.

Conserving, increasing, and transforming the chi energy should be the primary preventive method practiced. If you have had a heart attack, you can use this method to prevent a second. If you develop a bad kidney or bad back, you can use this method to prevent it from getting worse. In the Taoist system we map out all the organ energy meridians, which have a network extending from the organs throughout the body. When the flow of energy in the meridians is blocked or decreased, the organs will get less life force, and bad chi (that is, the chi we know as sick energy) will be trapped in the organs or the meridians.

If we are not in touch with our inner selves, it is very hard to notice these internal changes. But once we learn how to conserve, transform, and increase the chi, we have more chi to open the blockages, increase the body's defensive powers, and prevent illness. We can live the happy, healthy life we want to live and maintain our health as we age. Instead of going from one illness to another, we can have lifelong vitality and a positive will (desire) to live.

The Taoist system is geared to help you live a healthy life, free from illness, with vitality to help your fellow human beings. As we live our lives now, our attachment to the material world grows, and we become more and more drawn to material things, including various drugs, entertainment, services, and unnatural foods. The more we feel that we need to have this and buy that, the more worry and mixed emotions we feel. We can get rid of all of these feelings by getting rid of our emotional attachment to these things. When the organs and senses have sufficient healthy chi, they become strong and the need for external stimuli decreases. Many of my students have found it easy to give up coffee, drinks, drugs, and other kinds of "necessary" entertainment after using this system to work on themselves.

I have one student who previously owned a factory and was responsible for managing many workers. At the same time he was deeply in debt because he couldn't give up endlessly buying things. Finally, he came to me and talked to me about his problem. I explained to him that stress and emotional energy had created blockages and energy imbalances in his organs. If he could strengthen his organs and senses and increase the circulation in his body, he would see the world from a different angle. After he completed the Microcosmic Orbit meditation and practiced the Six Healing Sounds, Inner Smile, and Tao Rejuvenation, he came to me and said, "Master Chia, I'm going on a long vacation." I asked, "What happened?" He replied that he had sold his factory, paid all of his debts, and had a few thousand dollars left. "I want to rest, practice more of what you teach, and come back and start all over again," he said. There was a tremendous change in his face.

YOUR OWN HEALTH IS YOUR BEST INVESTMENT

Many people put all their life force into earning money, until their vitalities are depleted and illnesses set in. They have to spend more and more of their money on hospitals, surgery, medicine, and, finally, spend most of their time in bed.

Many people say, "I don't have time to practice. My day is filled with appointments and work, meetings, study, and children." But if you can improve your mind, body, and spiritual level of energy, your mind will be clearer; you will be more physically fit; your work will usually take less time to accomplish; and your emotions will be calmer.

Many of my students have the same problem: it is hard to find time to practice the Microcosmic Orbit, Six Healing Sounds, Inner Smile, Tao Rejuvenation, Tai Chi, Chi Kung, Iron Shirt, and Fusion of the Five Elements. These practices do take time to learn in the beginning, but after you learn them, they become part of your life. For example, you can do the Inner Smile while waiting in line. We spend a lot of time each day just waiting, and you can turn that time into practice time.

After studying this system for a while, many of our students find that they actually sleep less and eat less, so they end up having more time to do the practices. My knowledge and experience tell me that if people can make a thirty- to sixty-minute investment in their health each day, they will get one to four hours back, as well as be able to achieve more in less time. As a result, they will have more time to do more things.

TAOISM IN THE HOME

Taoists do not regard differing characteristics or personal qualities of a husband and wife as the main sources of unhappiness in a family. The natural thing is for opposites to attract each other. The most important thing is for the partners to understand each other, look at each other's strong points, and help to overcome each other's weak points.

In order to understand another person, you have to understand yourself first. The best way to understand yourself is to get in touch with your own organs. You can then strengthen your organs in order to transform negative energy and cultivate positive emotions and values.

Negative emotions are the main causes of energy imbalance in the body. The existence of negative energy in one family member will create negative emotions in other family members and disturb the energy balance in the entire family.

Sexual Imbalances Can Be Modified with Practice

Another factor in the breakdown of the family is an imbalance in the sex life of the married couple. Healthy vitality is a major source of sexual energy. The organs and glands are the main source of sexual energy, and therefore, healthy organs and glands will increase the happiness of a couple's sex life. A stressful life, pollution, and the vast regulations that govern life in our society rob people of their organ energies. They are left depressed, with their vitality and sexual energy depleted. This leads to psychological and marital problems. These problems can cause muscular weaknesses, such as impotence (inadequate erection) in men and lack of muscle tone in the sexual organs of women. For a couple, the question is how to increase and transform their sexual energies and therefore correct the physiological problems of the sexual organs. In this book we deal directly with strengthening the internal organs and senses.

Peacefulness of Chi Energy

The balance of peaceful chi energy in a person is very important because it can help to balance the chi of other people who are close. Five types of peace are necessary in a family:

Peace of Mind

Peace of the Heart

Peace of the Body

Peace of the Organs

Peace of the Senses

Taoism says that anything that is overly extreme will cause an imbalance of chi energy and will destroy peacefulness. Too much noise will hurt the ears and their associated organs, including the kidneys and the bladder, causing fear and disturbing the peace. Too much drinking or eating will hurt the spleen and indirectly hurt the liver, which will result in anger and bad temper and will disturb the peace of the family. Too much looking at television or movies will hurt the eyes, which will hurt the liver and the gallbladder and cause a loss of energy, weakening the vitality of the entire body. Too much exercise or overwork will hurt the tendons. Too much worry will hurt the nervous system.

Weakness of the organs or senses and nerves can cause certain types of unpleasant personal characteristics and bad habits, which can cause problems for the entire family in the long run. When a family understands the sources of the problems and uses the Taoist practices of the Inner Smile, Six Healing Sounds, and the Tao Rejuvenation exercises and meditations, they can treat the chi energy imbalances and organ weaknesses of family members. When one person comes down with a sickness due to stress or negative emotional energy, other members of the family can help to balance that energy before further problems develop. By practicing together, the energies of the family members are exchanged and balanced together as a family unit.

The Six Healing Sounds

THEORY AND BENEFITS

Thousands of years ago Taoist masters discovered that a healthy organ vibrates at a particular frequency. Their meditations also revealed six sounds with the correct frequencies to keep the organs in optimal condition to prevent and alleviate illness. Over time, six postures were developed to accompany the Six Healing Sounds, in order to activate the acupuncture meridians, or energy channels, of the organs (fig. 2.1 on pages 10 and 11).

There are twelve main meridians or channels, each named after one of the internal organs identified by traditional Chinese medicine. In addition, there are two special meridians that run along the center of the body. They are the Ren Mai or Functional Channel (on the front) and the Du Mai or Governor Channel (on the crown and back).

Overheating of the Organs

Organs malfunction for many reasons. Life in an urban society is full of physical and emotional stresses such as overcrowding, pollution, radiation, junk food, chemical additives, anxiety, loneliness, bad posture, and

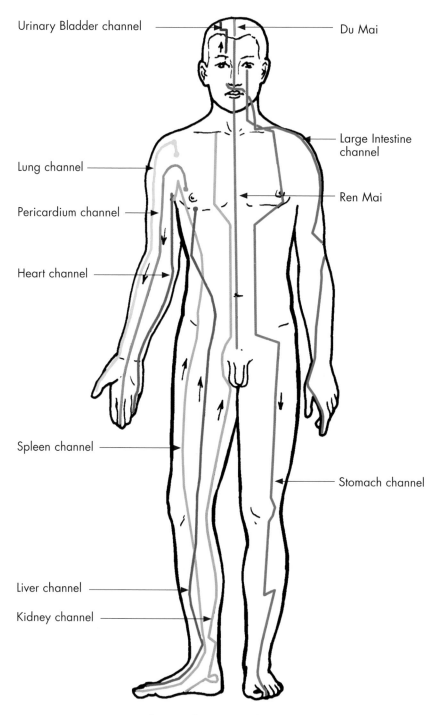

Urinary Bladder channel

Du Mai

Large Intestine channel

Lung channel

Ren Mai

Pericardium channel

Heart channel

Spleen channel

Stomach channel

Liver channel

Kidney channel

Fig. 2.1. Distribution of Fourteen Channels: Anterior View

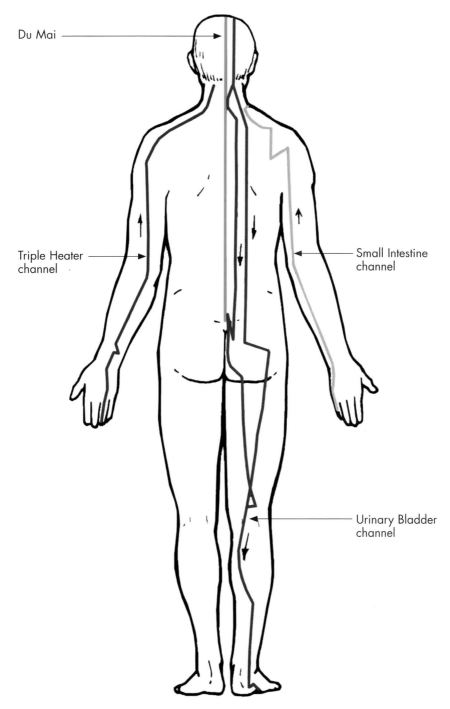

Du Mai

Triple Heater
channel

Small Intestine
channel

Urinary Bladder
channel

Fig. 2.1 (cont.). Posterior View

sudden or overly vigorous exercise. All kinds of waves stimulate our bodies and organs to hyperactivity. In addition, the "concrete jungle" that we live in lacks the safety valves provided by nature: trees, open spaces, and running water, which give forth a cooling, purifying energy. The circulation of our life-force energy becomes obstructed and unable to flow efficiently or easily.

When negative energy cannot be expelled from the body, it is circulated and trapped in the organs. Continued overheating causes an organ to contract and harden. This impairs its ability to function and results in illness. One of the surgeons working with the Universal Tao Center in New York reports that the hearts of patients who have died of heart attacks look as if they've been cooked! And the ancient Taoists have a saying: "Stress cooks your brain."

Cooling System of the Organs

Chinese medicine teaches that each organ is surrounded by a sac or membrane, called fascia, which regulates its temperature. Ideally, the membrane releases excess heat out through the skin, where it is exchanged for cool life-force energy from nature. An overload of physical or emotional tension causes the membrane, or fascia, to stick to the organ so that it cannot properly release heat to the skin nor absorb cool energy from the skin (fig. 2.2).

The skin becomes clogged with toxins until toxic deposits on tissues and muscles block the free passage of heat generated by the organs. The heat is reflected back into the organs, causing pressure, overheating, and eventual malfunction (fig. 2.3).

The Six Healing Sounds speed up the heat exchange through the digestive system and the mouth. The digestive system is more than twenty feet long and runs from the mouth to the anus like a pipe in the middle of the body, going in between all the organs. As the sound is made, the heat given off by the organs is transferred out of the body through the esophagus. This helps release excess heat from the fascia, thus cooling and cleansing the organs and skin.

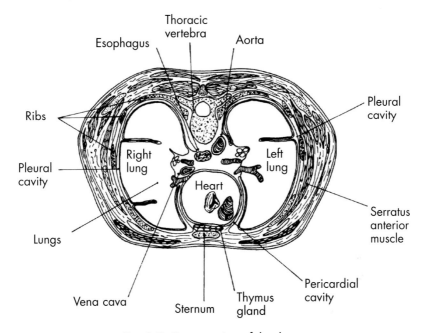

Fig. 2.2. Cross section of the thorax

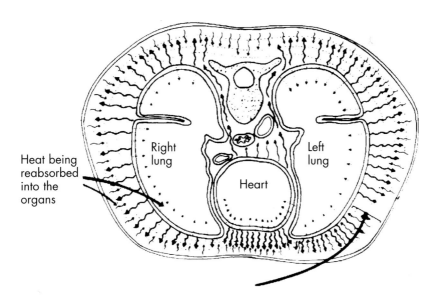

Fig. 2.3. Overheating of the organs

Esophagus

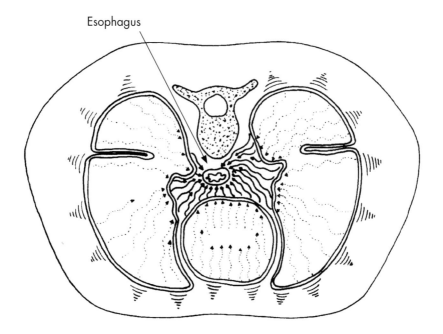

Fig. 2.4. Cooling system of the organs

When all the sounds and postures are done in the proper order, the heat of the body is evenly distributed by the intestinal tract, and each of the organs regains its correct temperature (fig. 2.4).

Each of the five organs in the practice has an associate organ, which responds together with it and in the same manner. When an organ is weak or overheated, its paired organ is similarly affected. Likewise, practicing the appropriate healing sound and posture improves the organ and its associate.

SOUNDS THAT HEAL
AND PREVENT

Daily practice of the Six Healing Sounds will restore and maintain calmness and good health. Greater sexual pleasure and improved digestion will occur. Minor ailments, such as colds, flu, and sore throats, can be prevented or thrown off easily. Many students of the Universal Tao system have overcome their long-standing dependence on sleeping pills, tranquilizers, aspirin, and antacids. Heart attack victims have prevented further attacks.

Several psychologists have taught some of their patients to use the Six Healing Sounds to relieve depression, anxiety, or anger. When the organ sounds are pronounced, the gas trapped in the organs is released and exchanged. The fresh energy releases or transforms negative emotions into more positive or life-giving energy. Bodywork healers have also used the Six Healing Sounds to help speed up healing, while requiring less of the healer's own life-force energy.

Sounds Can Increase the Range of Movement

A study done by Dr. G. Goodheart, the originator of a practice called Applied Kinesiology, showed that each large muscle was related to an organ of the body. A weakness in a muscle usually meant there was a problem in the chi energy level of its corresponding organ. In the Taoist system, all organs are associated with movement and the extremities. If there is an obstruction of energy in an organ, trapped bad energy, or negative emotions, movement of the muscles paired with that organ will be tense, painful, and limited. The muscles are like the back-up tank of the organs. So the range of movement throughout the body will be greatly obstructed and limited when the organs are obstructed with tension or under stress.

However, the Six Healing Sounds release the trapped energy in the organs. We find that many of our students improve their range of movement when the tensions are released from within their internal organs by practice of the Six Healing Sounds.

The chart on page 16 shows the details of the organs, muscles, and emotions associated with them (fig. 2.5).

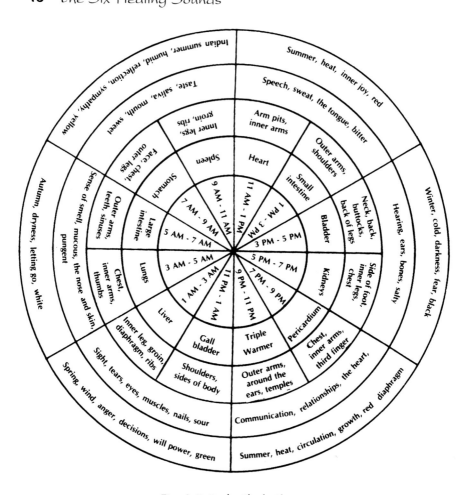

Fig. 2.5. Body Clock Chart

The times shown at the center of the body clock indicate the times of the day the individual organs and their respective channels have the most chi. Moving outward from the organs, the chart shows the linked areas of the body; then the associated senses, body substances, and tastes; and finally the related seasons, emotions, and colors.

The Best Detoxification Method Is Your Own Life-force Energy

People spend a lot of money for herbs and drugs in order to cleanse and detoxify their organs. However, substances often enter and remain in the system, causing more toxicity. Detoxification can be accomplished much more effectively by practicing the Six Healing Sounds. It is by far one of the best ways to clean out your organs, because it employs fresh energy to strengthen them and release the trapped gases that cause symptoms such as body odor and bad breath.

Mouth odor is a most common problem. Many people are not aware of how greatly it affects them personally. People who come in contact with someone with bad breath feel uncomfortable and unpleasant. When you know your breath is bad and you cannot get rid of the persistent odor, you gradually lose confidence in yourself in social gatherings. One of the reasons for bad breath is tooth decay, which can be corrected by a dentist. The other major cause of bad breath is unhealthy internal organs. A sickly liver, for example, will cause bad breath that smells like decaying meat. When the kidneys are not in a healthy state, they will cause the breath to smell like fermented urine. A weak or sickly stomach is the main cause of bad breath. When the healthy digestive activities of the stomach and the intestines are interfered with, a great accumulation of partially undigested food remains in their walls, leading to bad breath.

Strong body odors also make people disliked, especially in the summer. Body odor can be caused by long-term work under stress, which makes the organs more nervous and can cause organ pain, especially stomach pain. Stomach pain obstructs the digestive system and the chi circulatory system. The odor that is secreted in perspiration, especially the odor secreted by the armpits (which tap the body's energy flow), then becomes very strong. The Six Healing Sounds, especially the lungs' sound, can aid energy circulation. To do the lungs' sound you have to raise your hands above your head and expose your armpits. This will help to exchange the energy in the armpits so that the organs are more open and cleaner.

The kidneys' sound also helps to eliminate bad perspiration. People who perspire easily, with little movement or when nervous, do so because they have weak kidneys, which are not able to filter the uric acid out of the body and into the bloodstream. When this filtering system breaks down, an excess build-up of uric acid occurs in the kidneys and throughout the body. Then, the body becomes stressed and fear occurs easily, reflecting in foul-smelling perspiration. Uttering the kidneys' sound and massaging the kidney area in the back with light tapping can help to shake the stuck uric acid particles loose from the kidney filters. Massaging the feet, especially at the Bubbling Spring points on the soles of the feet, will also help greatly.

Side Effects of Detoxification

During or shortly after doing the Six Healing Sounds, it is common to experience yawning, moving of gas, or other mild symptoms. Some people may experience loose or very bad smelling bowel movements. These are all indications of ongoing detoxification. Although yawning, burping, and passing gas aren't socially approved responses in North America, they are actually beneficial. They're part of the process of releasing trapped bad breath, gas, and hot energy from the digestive system. As you inhale, you take cool fresh life-force energy into your esophagus. Exhaling and pronouncing the correct sound creates an exchange of energy, bringing the good energy to the organ and forcing out the waste energy. The world now spends billions of dollars on antacids to release trapped gas. The Six Healing Sounds do the same thing more efficiently and without expense.

The practice of the Six Healing Sounds may also cause other signs of detoxification to develop, such as tearing. Tearing helps prevent eye disease and cleanses the organs. Cleaning out your system will also usually be followed by a spring of saliva from the glands of your mouth, which you will feel to be fresh and fragrant. When you have a lot of saliva, swallow down by pressing your tongue to the roof of your mouth, locking your neck, and swallowing.

PREPARATION FOR THE SIX HEALING SOUNDS

For maximum benefit, be precise in assuming the position and making the sound for each organ. During all of the exhalation positions, you will be looking up at the ceiling with your head tilted back. This creates a straight path from your open mouth, through your esophagus, down to your organs, permitting a more efficient exchange of energy.

All sounds should be made slowly and evenly. At first, you can produce the sounds aloud, but eventually you should practice subvocally (vocalizing so softly that only you can hear the sound). The sounds are formed with the lips, teeth, and tongue, but they are heard only internally; this intensifies their power.

Be sure to follow the order of the exercises as given. This enhances the even distribution of heat in the body. The order follows the natural order of the seasons, from autumn through winter, spring, summer, and Indian summer (a period of unusually warm weather after summer).

Wait at least an hour after eating to begin the practice. However, if you have gas, nausea, or stomach cramps you may do just the spleen's sound right after eating.

Choose a quiet spot and turn off your phone. Until you've developed a strong inner focus, you need to eliminate distractions.

Dress warmly enough not to be chilled. Wear loose fitting clothes and loosen your belt. Remove your glasses and watch.

Sit on your sitz bones at the edge of a chair. Your genitals (an important energy center) should be unsupported. Your legs should be hip width apart, and your feet should be solidly on the floor. Keep your back straight and shoulders relaxed; sink your chest (fig. 2.6).

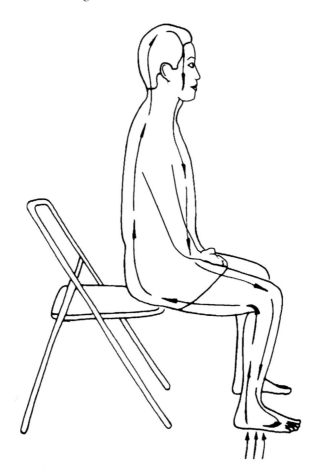

Fig. 2.6. The proper position for beginning to practice

Keep your eyes open.

Rest your hands in your lap. You are now ready to begin the exercises.

The Six Healing Sounds exercises can also be done while standing. Instructions for the standing positions are given in chapter four, "Supplementary Practices."

Lung Exercise: First Healing Sound

Characteristics

Associated Organ: Large intestine
Element: Metal
Season: Autumn (dryness)
Negative Emotions: Grief, sadness, depression, sorrow
Positive Emotions: Courage, righteousness, justice, detachment
Sound: Sss-s-s-s-s (tongue behind teeth)
Parts of the Body: Chest, inner arms, thumbs
Sense/Body Substance: Smell, nose, mucus, skin
Taste: Pungent
Color: White

Position and Practice

1. Become aware of your lungs as you rest your hands on your thighs, with your palms up (fig. 2.7).
2. Take a deep breath and raise your arms up in front of you, letting your eyes follow them. When your hands are at eye level, begin to rotate your palms and bring them up above your head. Keep your elbows rounded. You should feel a stretch that extends from the heels of the palms, along the forearms, over the elbows, along the upper arms, and into the shoulders. Your lungs and chest will feel open and breathing will be easier (figs. 2.8 and 2.9).
3. Close your jaws so that your teeth meet gently, and part your lips slightly. Draw the corners of your mouth back, exhale, and allow your breath to escape through the spaces between the teeth, subvocally making the sound "sss-s-s-s-s," (like the sound of steam coming from a radiator), slowly and evenly in one breath (fig. 2.10).
4. As you exhale slowly and fully, picture and feel the pleura (the sacs surrounding the lungs) being fully compressed, ejecting the excess heat, sick energy, sadness, sorrow, and grief (fig. 2.11).

5. When you have exhaled completely (without straining), rotate your palms down, close your eyes, and breathe in to the lungs to strengthen them. If you are color oriented, you can imagine a pure white light entering into your lungs, along with the quality of righteousness. Float your arms down by gently lowering your shoulders. Slowly lower your hands to your lap so that they rest there, palms up. Feel the energy exchange in your hands and palms.

6. Close your eyes, breathe normally, and be aware of your lungs. Smile down to them and imagine that you are still making the lungs' sound. Pay attention to any sensations you may feel. Try to feel the exchange of cool, fresh energy replacing hot waste energy (fig. 2.12).

7. When your breathing calms down, repeat the sequence 3 to 6 times.

8. For colds, flu, mucus, toothaches, smoking, asthma, emphysema, or depression, or if you want to increase the range of movement of your chest and inner arm, or to detoxify the lungs, you can repeat the sound 9, 12, 18, 24, or 36 times.

9. The lungs' sound can also help to eliminate nervousness when in front of a crowd. You can do the lungs' sound subvocally without the hand movements several times when you feel nervous. This will help you to calm down. The heart's sound and the Inner Smile will also help if the lungs' sound is not sufficiently calming.

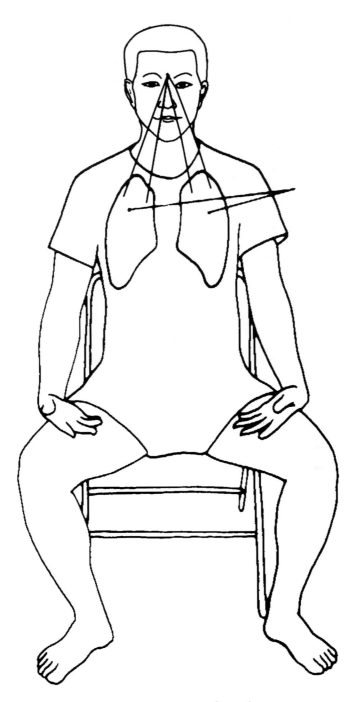

Fig. 2.7. Become aware of your lungs.

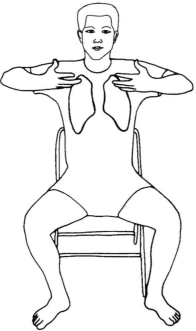

Fig. 2.8. Rotate your palms and . . .

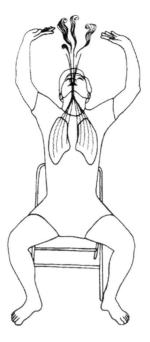

Fig. 2.9. . . . bring them up above your head.

Fig. 2.10. Mouth position for lungs' sound.
Close jaws so that the teeth meet. Draw the corners of the mouth back.

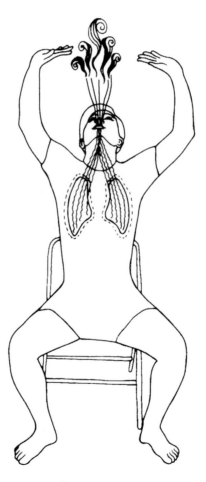

Fig. 2.11. Picture and feel the sacs being fully compressed.

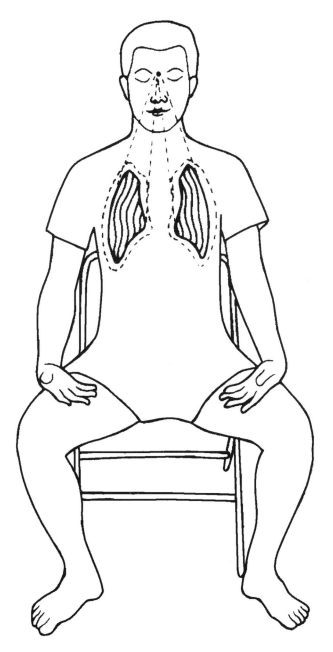

Fig. 2.12. Close your eyes; breathe normally;
smile down to your lungs.

Kidney Exercise: Second Healing Sound

Characteristics

Associated Organ: Urinary Bladder

Element: Water

Season: Winter

Negative Emotion: Fear, shock

Positive Emotions: Gentleness, alertness, stillness, gratitude

Sound: Choo-oo-oo-oo (as when blowing out a candle with the lips forming an "O")

Parts of the Body: Side of foot, inner legs, chest

Sense/Body Substance: Hearing, ears, bones

Taste: Salty

Color: Blue or black

Position and Practice

1. Become aware of your kidneys (fig. 2.13).

2. Place your legs together, ankles and knees touching. Take a deep breath as you bend forward, clasp one hand in the other, hook your hands around your knees, and pull back on your arms. With your arms straight, feel the pull at the back where the kidneys are; look up, and tilt your head back without straining (fig. 2.14).

3. Round your lips and silently make the sound made when blowing out a candle. At the same time, press your middle abdomen, between the sternum and navel, toward your spine. Imagine the excess heat, wet, sick energy, and fear being squeezed out from the membrane around your kidneys (figs. 2.15, 2.16, and 2.17).

4. When you have exhaled completely, sit up and slowly breathe into the kidneys, imagining a bright blue energy as the quality of gentleness enters the kidneys. Separate your legs and rest your hands, palms up, on your thighs.

5. Close your eyes and breathe normally. Smile to your kidneys, as you imagine that you are still making the sound. Pay attention to

sensations. Be aware of the exchange of energy around the kidneys, hands, head, and legs (fig. 2.18).

6. When your breathing calms down, repeat 3 to 6 times.

7. For back pain, fatigue, dizziness, ringing in the ears, or detoxifying the kidneys, repeat 9 to 36 times.

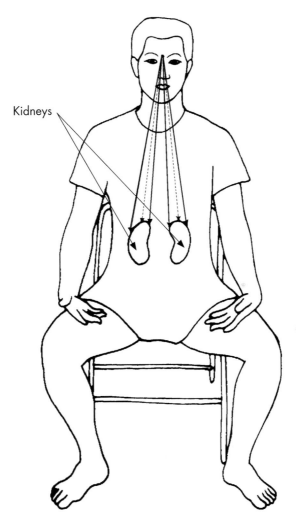

Kidneys

Fig. 2.13. Become aware of your kidneys.

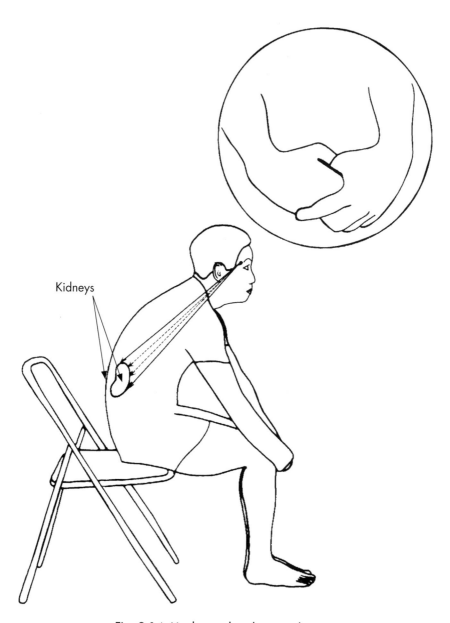

Kidneys

Fig. 2.14. Hook your hands around your
knees as you look up and pull.

Fig. 2.14 (cont.). Hook your hands around
your knees as you look up and pull.

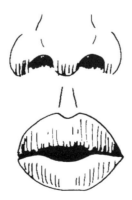

Fig. 2.15. Round the lips, forming an "O."

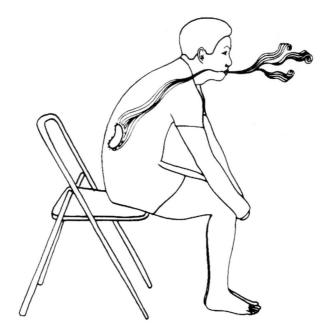

Fig. 2.16. With lips rounded, silently make the sound one makes when blowing out a candle.

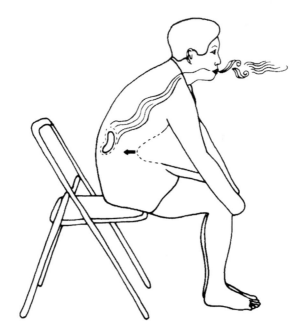

Fig. 2.17. Press the middle abdomen toward the kidneys.

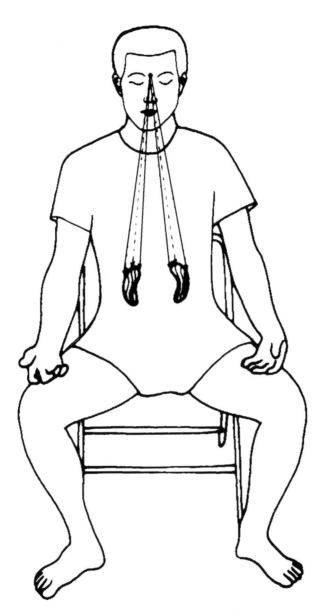

Fig. 2.18. Close your eyes and
smile down to your kidneys.

Liver Exercise: Third Healing Sound

Characteristics

Associated Organ: Gallbladder

Element: Wood

Season: Spring

Negative Emotions: Anger, aggression

Positive Emotions: Kindness, generosity, forgiveness, self-expansion, identity

Sound: Sh-h-h-h-h-h-h (tongue near palate)

Parts of the Body: Inner legs, groin, diaphragm, ribs

Sense/Body Substance: Sight, eyes, tears

Taste: Sour

Color: Green

Position and Practice

1. Become aware of the liver, and feel the connection between the eyes and the liver (fig. 2.19).

2. Place your arms at your sides, palms out. Take a deep breath as you slowly swing your arms up and over your head. Follow with your eyes (fig. 2.20).

3. Interlace your fingers and rotate your palms to face the ceiling (fig. 2.21). Push out at the heels of your palms and feel the stretch through your arms and into your shoulders. Bend slightly to the left, exerting a gentle pull on the liver (fig. 2.22).

4. Open your eyes wide and exhale the sound, "sh-h-h-h-h-h-h" subvocally (fig. 2.23). Envision and feel the expulsion of excess heat and anger from the liver as the fascia around it compresses (fig. 2.24).

5. When you have exhaled completely, unlock your fingers. Pressing out with the heels of your palms, breathe into the liver slowly and imagine a bright green color and quality of kindness entering the liver. Gently bring your arms down to your sides by lowering your shoulders (fig. 2.25). Place your hands on your lap, palms up, and rest.

6. Close your eyes, breathe normally, smile down to your liver, and imagine you are still making the sound. Be aware of sensations. Sense the energy exchange (fig. 2.26).

7. Do this 3 to 6 times. For anger, red and watery eyes, or a sour or bitter taste, and for detoxifying the liver, repeat 9 to 36 times.

A Taoist axiom about controlling anger says: If you've done the liver sound 30 times and you are still angry at someone, you have the right to slap that person.

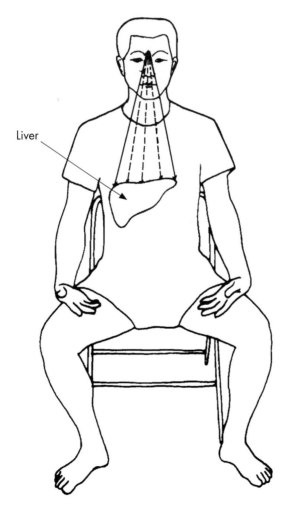

Fig. 2.19. Become aware of your liver.

Fig. 2.20. Slowly swing your arms up and over your head.

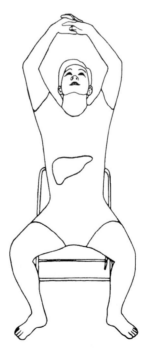

Fig. 2.21. Interlace your fingers and rotate your palms.

Fig. 2.22. Push out at the heels of your palms.
Push more with your right arm.

Fig. 2.23. Exhale on the sound "sh-h-h-h-h-h-h."

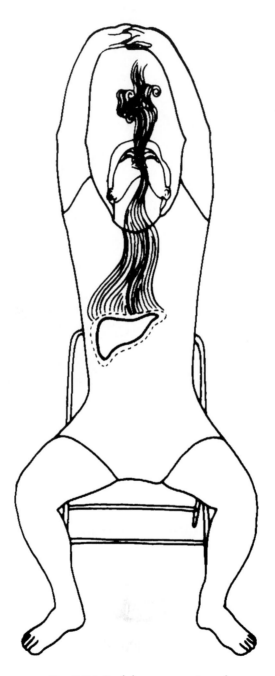

Fig. 2.24. Feel the compression of
the fascia enclosing the liver.

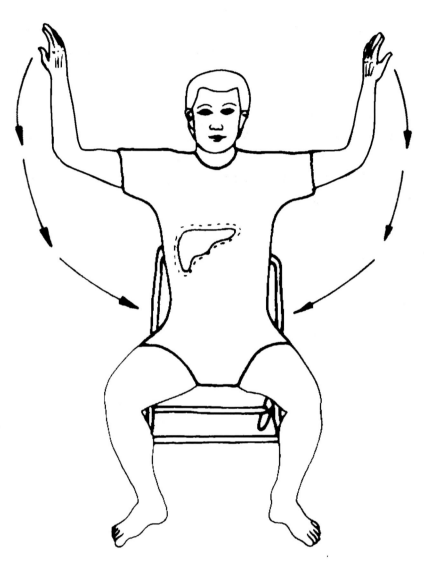

Fig. 2.25. Press out with the heels of the palms.

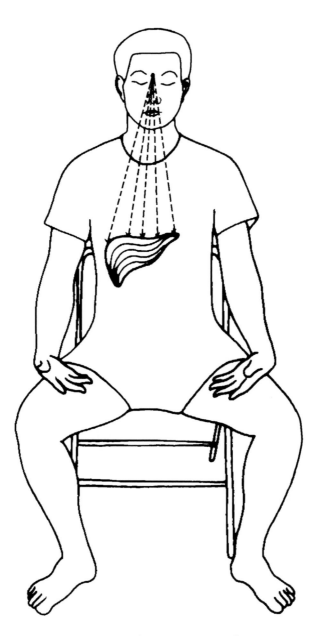

Fig. 2.26. Close your eyes and
smile down to your liver.

Heart Exercise: Fourth Healing Sound

Characteristics

Associated Organ: Small Intestine

Element: Fire

Season: Summer

Negative Emotions: Impatience, arrogance, hastiness, cruelty, violence

Positive Emotions: Love, joy, happiness, honor, sincerity, creativity, enthusiasm

Sound: Haw-w-w-w-w-w (mouth wide open)

Parts of the Body: Armpits, inner arms

Sense/Body Substance: Tongue, speech, sweat

Taste: Bitter

Color: Red

The heart is constantly working, beating at the rate of approximately 72 times a minute, 4,320 times an hour, 102,680 times each day. This naturally produces heat, which is dissipated by the heart's sac, the pericardium. In the Taoist view, the pericardium is important enough to be considered a separate organ.

Position and Practice

1. Become aware of your heart and feel the connection between your tongue and heart (fig. 2.27).
2. Take a deep breath and assume the same position as for the liver's sound (fig. 2.28), but lean slightly to the right (fig. 2.29).
3. Open your mouth, round your lips, and slowly exhale the sound "haw-w-w-w-w-w" subvocally (fig. 2.30). Breathe out the dark, murky energy as you picture the pericardium expelling heat, impatience, arrogance, and hastiness (figs. 2.31 and 2.32).

4. For the rest cycle, repeat the procedure for the liver's sound, but focus attention on your heart and smile down to it. Imagine a bright red color and the qualities of love, joy, honor, sincerity, and creativity entering your heart (fig. 2.33).

5. Repeat 3 to 6 times. For a sore throat, cold sores, swollen gums or tongue, heart disease, heart pains, jumpiness, moodiness, and for detoxifying the heart, repeat 9 to 36 times.

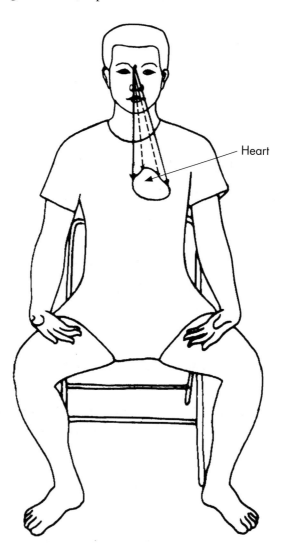

Heart

Fig. 2.27. Become aware of your heart.

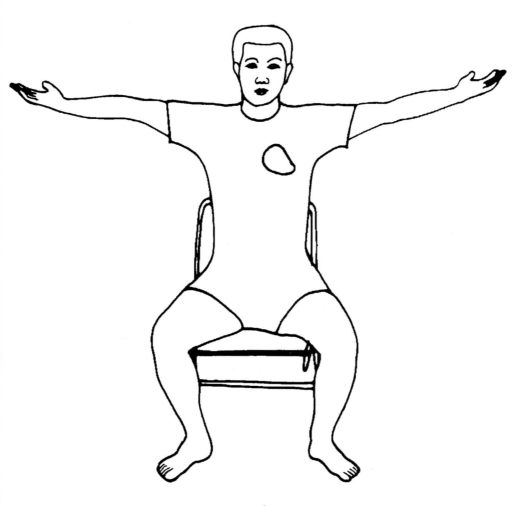

Fig. 2.28. Assume the same position
as for the liver's sound.

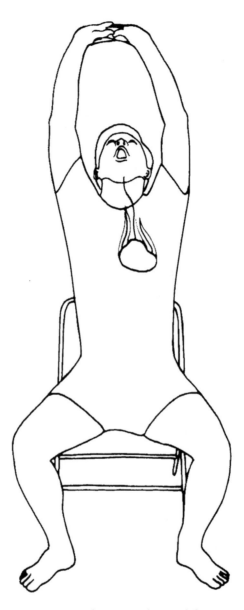

Fig. 2.29. Push more with your left arm.

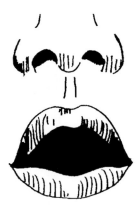

Fig. 2.30. Open your mouth, round your lips, and exhale the sound "haw-w-w-w-w-w."

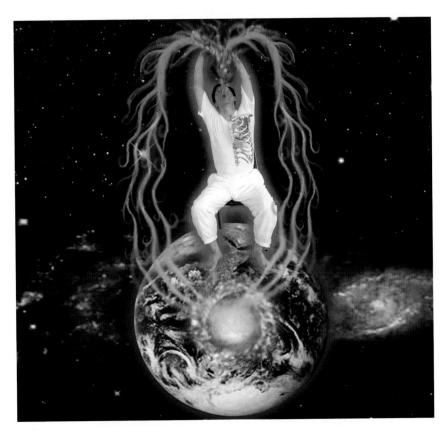

Fig. 2.31. Breathe out the dark, murky energy.

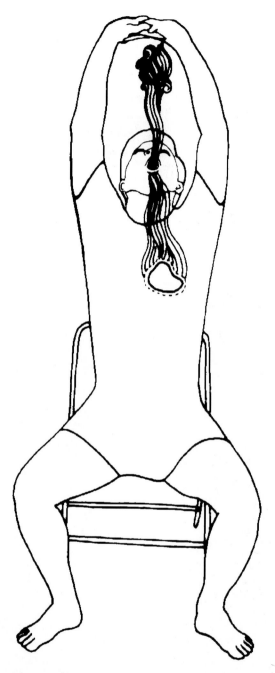

Fig. 2.32. Picture the pericardium expelling heat, impatience, arrogance, and hastiness.

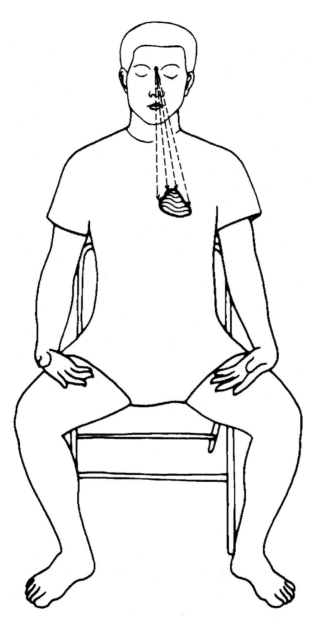

Fig. 2.33. Close your eyes and
smile down to your heart.

Spleen Exercise: Fifth Healing Sound

Characteristics

Associated Organs: Pancreas, stomach

Element: Earth

Season: Indian summer

Negative Emotions: Worry, anxiety, pity

Positive Emotions: Fairness, openness, compassion, centering, balance

Sound: Who-o-o-o-o-o (from the throat, guttural)

Parts of the Body: Inner legs, groin, ribs

Sense/Body Substance: Taste, mouth, saliva

Taste: Sweet

Color: Yellow

Position and Practice

1. Become aware of your spleen; feel your mouth and spleen connect (fig. 2.34).
2. Take a deep breath as you place the fingers of both hands just beneath the sternum on your left side (fig. 2.35). Press in with your fingers as you push your middle back outward (fig. 2.36).
3. Exhale on the sound "who-o-o-o-o-o" made subvocally and felt in the vocal chords (figs. 2.37 and 2.38). Expel the excess heat, dampness, worry, and pity.
4. Breathe into your spleen, pancreas, and stomach (fig. 2.39). Imagine a bright yellow light entering them, along with the qualities of fairness, compassion, and centering.
5. Lower your hands slowly to your lap, palms up.
6. Close your eyes and breathe normally as you smile down to your spleen, pancreas, and stomach. Imagine you are still making the sound. Be aware of sensations and the exchange of energy (fig. 2.40).

7. Repeat 3 to 6 times.

8. Repeat 9 to 36 times for indigestion, nausea, and diarrhea, and for detoxifying the spleen. This sound, done in conjunction with the others, is more effective and healthier than using antacids. It is the only sound that can be done immediately after eating.

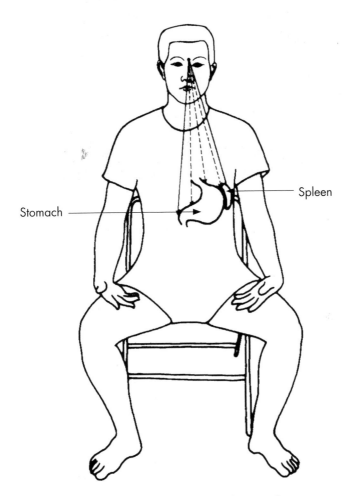

Fig. 2.34. Become aware of your spleen.

Fig. 2.35. Take a deep breath and place the fingers
of both hands just beneath the sternum on your left side.

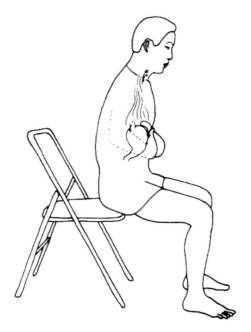

Fig. 2.36. Press in with your fingers and
push your middle back outward.

Fig. 2.37. Exhale on the sound "who-o-o-o-o-o."

Fig. 2.38. Feel the sound in your vocal chords as you
expel excess heat, dampness, worry, and pity.

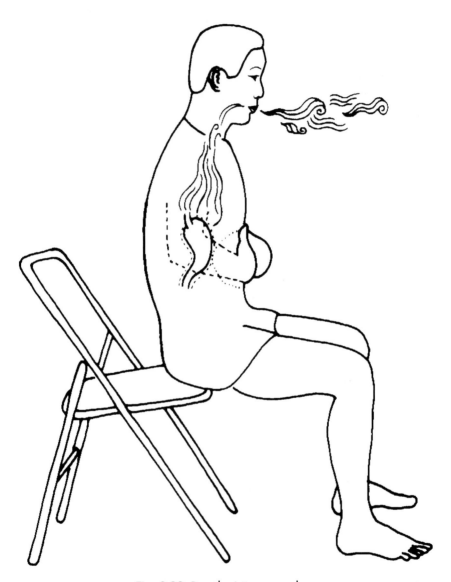

Fig. 2.39. Breathe into your spleen,
pancreas, and stomach.

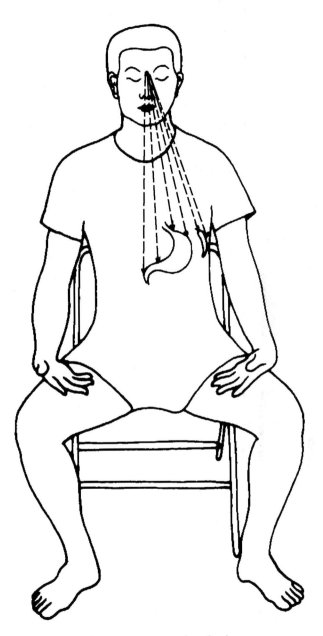

Fig. 2.40. Close your eyes and smile down to your
spleen, pancreas, and stomach.

Triple Heater Exercise: Sixth Healing Sound

Characteristics

The Triple Heater (also referred to as the Triple Warmer) does not have the same characteristics as the other five organs as it comprises the three energy centers of the body (fig. 2.41).

The upper level, which consists of the brain, heart, and lungs, is hot.

The middle section, consisting of the liver, kidneys, stomach, pancreas, and spleen, is warm.

The lower level, containing the large and small intestines, the bladder, and the sexual organs, is cool.

The Triple Heater's sound "he-e-e-e-e-e" balances the temperature of the three levels by bringing hot energy down to the lower center and cold energy up to the upper center through the digestive tract. This induces a deep, relaxing sleep. A number of students have been able to break a long-standing dependence on sleeping pills by practicing this sound. It is also very effective for relieving stress.

There is no season, color, or emotion associated with the Triple Heater.

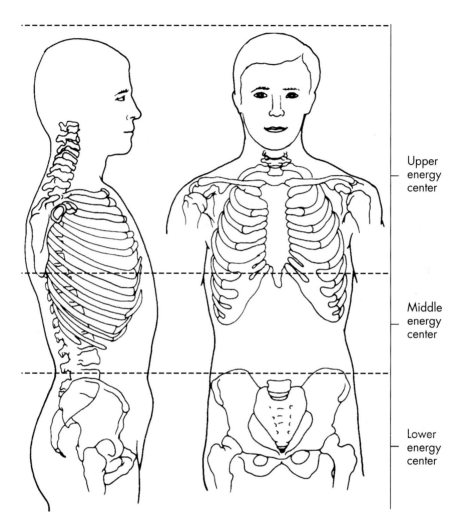

Upper
energy
center

Middle
energy
center

Lower
energy
center

Fig. 2.41. Triple Heater

● Position and Practice

1. Lie down on your back, close your eyes, and take a deep breath (fig. 2.42). Elevate your knees with a pillow if you feel any pain in the small of your back or lumbar area.

2. As you breathe in, expand your stomach and chest without strain (fig. 2.43).

3. Inhale fully into all three levels (figs. 2.44, 2.45, 2.46, and 2.47).

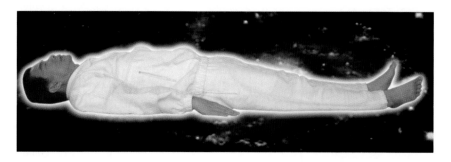

Fig. 2.42. Lie on your back, close your eyes, and take a deep breath.

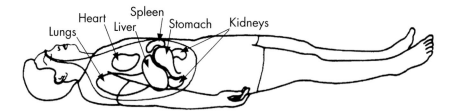

Fig. 2.43. Organ diagram

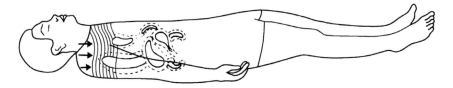

Fig. 2.44. Breathe into upper section.

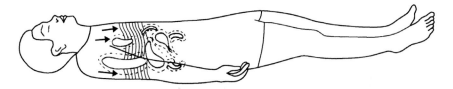

Fig. 2.45. Breathe into middle section.

Fig. 2.46. Breathe into lower section.

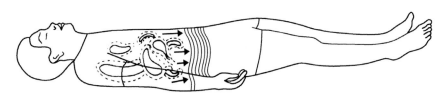

Fig. 2.47. Breathe into everything.

4. Exhale on the sound "he-e-e-e-e-e" made subvocally (fig. 2.48), as you picture and feel a large roller pressing out your breath, beginning at the top of your chest and ending at your lower abdomen. Imagine your chest and abdomen are as flat as a sheet of paper, and feel light, bright, and empty.

5. Rest by breathing normally (fig. 2.49).

6. Repeat 3 to 6 times, or more, if you are still wide awake. The Triple Heater's sound also can be used to relax, without falling asleep, by lying on your side or sitting in a chair.

Fig. 2.48. He-e-e-e-e-e sound

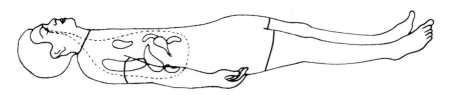

Fig. 2.49. Rest by breathing normally.

DAILY USE

Try to Practice the Six Healing Sounds Daily

Any time of the day is fine. This practice is especially effective when it is done at bedtime because it induces a deep, relaxing sleep. Once you have learned the procedure, it takes only 10 to 15 minutes.

Release the Heat after Vigorous Exercise

Do the Six Healing Sounds right after vigorous exercise, such as aerobics, jogging, martial arts, or after any type of yoga or meditation that creates a lot of heat in the upper energy center (the brain, lungs, or heart). This prevents the dangerous overheating of the organs that can otherwise occur. Do not take a cold shower right after vigorous exercise; it's too much of a shock to the organs.

Do the Sounds in Proper Sequence

1. Always do the sounds in the proper sequence: lungs' sound (autumn), kidneys' sound (winter), liver's sound (spring), heart's sound (summer), spleen's sound (Indian summer), Triple Heater's sound.
2. If a particular organ or its accompanying symptom is bothering you, increase the number of times you do that individual sound without going through the whole sequence.

Season, Organ, and Sound

An organ works harder, and thus creates more heat, during the season in which it is dominant. Therefore, increase the number of times you do its exercise in that season. For example, in spring do the liver's sound 6 to 9 times, while doing the other sounds 3 to 6 times.

If you are very pressed for time or very fatigued, only do the lung and kidney exercises.

Get in Touch During the Resting Period

The resting period after each sound is very important. This is the time that you get in touch with your organs and become more aware of them. When you rest and smile into a particular organ, you will often feel the exchange of the chi energy in the organ, the hands, and the legs. The head also feels the energy flow.

The sensations experienced during the rest periods vary from individual to individual. You may feel coolness, tingling, vibration, lightness, or expansion in a particular organ, or in your head, hands, or legs. Or you may feel nothing specific, just a general feeling of relaxation. You may begin to sense the changes as your organs become softer, moister, spongier, and more open.

Take as much time as you desire during the rest periods.

Taoist Wisdom for Daily Life

SMILE AWAY THE STRESS

It is common knowledge that life today is very hectic. Ending the workday with a headache has become a way of life for many. With pressures seemingly building all around and within you, "something has to be done." Oddly, the "thing to do" is not to do anything. No matter what kind of trying situation arises, you have to learn not to be drawn in by it. The way to accomplish that is to smile. In that simple act the world is made over, and what would otherwise have been troublesome will usually dissipate.

Remember always to smile sincerely with your eyes and to fill your heart with love. This acts as a preventive medicine, especially when you use the Inner Smile practice to smile to your own organs. When you are sad, angry, crying, depressed, or nervous, your organs secrete poisons, but when you are happy and smile, they produce a honey-like, health-giving secretion instead.

Wherever you are—standing, walking, or sitting—remember to smile and relax, to fill your heart with love and to let the loving feeling spread throughout your whole body. It is so very simple and yet so very effective. Just cultivate a peaceful, loving heart, smile easily, and your troubles will melt away.

CULTIVATING MENTAL POWER

Taoist methods involve the cultivation of generative and mental power. In Chinese and many other Oriental languages, the word for "mind" also means "heart." When you develop to the stage of no longer being concerned with personal ambition, when you are able to forget yourself and cultivate your heart, you have at hand the means of being free from illness.

When you are ill and meditate, do not think that you are doing it to escape from your illness. Instead, simply concentrate on a prescribed point or method and everything else will drop away.

MODERATION IN EVERYTHING

Walking too long harms the tendons; sitting too long harms the flesh; standing too long harms the bones; lying down too long harms vital energy; and gazing too long harms the blood.

Try not to use your senses too much. Don't look at or listen to anything for too long at a time. Whenever the senses are used excessively, sickness can result.

Anger, grief, pity, and melancholy are harmful, as are too much joy and pleasure. Suffering is harmful; abstinence from sexual activity is harmful; to be anxious is harmful. In short, to neglect moderation is harmful.

CONTROL YOUR SEX LIFE—DO NOT LET IT CONTROL YOU

Curb your sexual activity. You can exhaust your vital energy and reduce your ability to concentrate by too frequent sexual activity.

The mind is troubled by what is fed to it through the eyes, ears, mouth, nose, and mind—that is, the senses. When we are young and are exposed to sexually stimulating reading matter, we are not equipped to deal properly with it in a way that conserves our energy.

Therefore, it is advised that you concentrate on your daily practice and avoid "distractions."

WISDOM IN EATING

Overindulge yourself with too much food and drink, and you will cause yourself ill health.

Do not overeat until you are too full and then lie down or sit for a long time, as doing this will surely shorten your life.

Eat short of satiation and then take a leisurely stroll; do not eat at all at night before retiring.

Eat small amounts of food and eat more frequently. In this way you will be assured of proper digestion and of not overtaxing your organs.

When eating, eat hot foods first, then warm, then cold; if there is no cold food, drink some cold water. Always, before eating, inhale slightly and swallow some air.

Eat more pungent food in the spring, more sour food in the summer, more bitter food in autumn, and less salty food in winter, but do not be excessive in doing this.

In general, cooked food is better than uncooked, and eating a little is better than eating a lot.

If you have eaten too much, be careful not to drink too much water and not to gulp it down suddenly.

Indigestion follows when you eat to satiation after having been hungry for a long time.

Do not eat raw fruit on an empty stomach, because it heats above the diaphragm.

Too many raw vegetables can upset one's healthy color.

RESPECT YOUR HEAD—WARM YOUR FEET

Regard your head with the greatest respect. See it as the temple of the soul and the main control of all the vital organs. Abide by this simple rule of thumb: "Warm feet, cool head." Rub your feet to keep them warm. This will protect you from collecting too much power in your head, thereby possibly causing you discomfort or illness. When power goes to the head, high blood pressure can develop, but directing the power down to your feet can relieve the pressure. Keeping your feet warm can also guard you against heart attack.

It is also important to keep your neck warm, as it connects to your head and has many important blood vessels and nerves. So treat it well; keep it warm and loose by pervading it with a smile.

JOY INCREASES THE CHI

With great joy, the vital chi soars. Great sadness causes the flow of chi to stop.

Think less about the future and the past, because those are the things that worry builds on, and worry produces stress. Try instead to cultivate attitudes of helping and of forgiveness in your daily life.

SPEAK THOUGHTFULLY

Speak less; choose carefully what you say and when and how you say it. Speaking appropriately can be a blessing to all, and speaking less conserves chi.

SEASONAL HEALTH CARE

During winter, see to it that your feet are warm and allow your head to be cool. In the spring and autumn permit both your head and feet to be cool.

When lying down in spring and summer, your head should face east, whereas in autumn and winter it should face west.

In summer and autumn go to sleep early and arise early; in winter retire early and arise late; and in spring go to sleep while there is daylight and arise early.

DAILY HEALTH CARE

At dawn, midday, during the afternoon, at twilight, and at midnight, clean your teeth and rinse your mouth seven times; this will lengthen your life and strengthen your bones, teeth, muscles, nails, and hair.

To prolong your life and avoid illness, practice swallowing your saliva many times a day. To swallow saliva is to increase its essence. When it is not swallowed it loses strength.

Replace the unpurified chi of your body with pure original chi by practicing the Microcosmic Orbit.

Do not expose yourself to the wind after bathing or perspiring.

When sleeping, bend your knees and lie on your side. This increases your vital energy.

Right after awakening from sleep, avoid talking too much, as this will rob you of vital energy.

Men, to be free of sickness, squat to urinate before eating and stand to urinate after eating.

When ill and perspiring, do not drink cold water, as this will damage your heart and stomach.

When you are ill, do not lie with your head to the north.

Please the divinities within, and you may in time progress toward immortality.

4

Supplementary Practices: Standing Healing Sounds

The characteristics of the organs and the general instructions for the performance of the Six Healing Sounds given earlier should be kept in mind when doing the sounds in a standing position. Here, the practice of each sound begins with gathering energy.

 ## Standing Lungs' Sound

Fig. 4.1. Gather the energy.   Fig. 4.2. Focus on your lungs.

Fig. 4.3. Raise your hands
above your head.

Fig. 4.4. Draw head back.

Fig. 4.5. Make the lungs'
sound: "sss-s-s-s-s-s."

Fig. 4.6. Draw energy down.

Fig. 4.7. Gather energy at your navel.

Fig. 4.8. Smile into your lungs.

Fig. 4.9. Feel the white light
in your lungs.

Standing Kidneys' Sound

Fig. 4.10. Gather energy, cup knees, make kidneys' sound: "choo-oo-oo-oo."

Fig. 4.11. Draw back, cover kidneys.

Fig. 4.12. Breathe in blue healing energy.

Standing Liver's Sound

Fig. 4.13. Gather energy
for your liver.

Fig. 4.14. Raise your hands
above your head.

Fig. 4.15. Connect
your hands over
your head.

Fig. 4.16. Turn your
hands over, and
put head back.

Fig. 4.17. Make the liver's
sound: "sh-h-h-h-h-h-h."

Fig. 4.18. Release energy.

Fig. 4.19. Draw your hands down.

Fig. 4.20. Gather energy
into your liver.

Fig. 4.21. Cover your liver.

Standing Heart's Sound

Fig. 4.22. Draw your hands
to your heart.

Fig. 4.23. Gather energy.

Fig. 4.24. Draw your hands upward.

Fig. 4.25. Lift your hands
over your head.

Fig. 4.26. Connect your hands.

Fig. 4.27. Make the heart's sound: "haw-w-w-w-w-w."

Fig. 4.28. Release your hands.

Fig. 4.29. Draw your hands to your chest.

Fig. 4.30. Cover your heart.

Standing Spleen's Sound

Fig. 4.31. Cover your spleen.

Fig. 4.32. Gather energy.

Fig. 4.33. Draw your hands
into your spleen.

Fig. 4.34. Make the spleen's sound:
"who-o-o-o-o-o."

Fig. 4.35. Feel the bright
yellow energy.

Fig. 4.36. Cover
your spleen.

Standing Triple Heater's Sound

Fig. 4.37. Gather energy.

Fig. 4.38. Raise your hands
above your head.

Fig. 4.39. Lower your hands.

Fig. 4.40. Make the Triple Heater's sound: "he-e-e-e-e-e."

Fig. 4.41. Release the heat.

Fig. 4.42. Relax and breathe normally.

About the Author

Mantak Chia has been studying the Taoist approach to life since childhood. His mastery of this ancient knowledge, enhanced by his study of other disciplines, has resulted in the development of the Universal Tao System, which is now being taught throughout the world.

Mantak Chia was born in Thailand to Chinese parents in 1944. When he was six years old, he learned from Buddhist monks how to sit and "still the mind." While in grammar school he learned traditional Thai boxing, and soon went on to acquire considerable skill in Aikido, Yoga, and Tai Chi. His studies of the Taoist way of life began in earnest when he was a student in Hong Kong, ultimately leading to his mastery of a wide variety of esoteric disciplines, with the guidance of several masters, including Master I Yun, Master Meugi, Master Cheng Yao Lun, and Master Pan Yu. To better understand the mechanisms behind healing energy, he also studied Western anatomy and medical sciences.

Master Chia has taught his system of healing and energizing practices to tens of thousands of students and trained more than two thousand instructors and practitioners throughout the world. He has established centers for Taoist study and training in many countries around the globe. In June 1990 he was honored by the International Congress of Chinese Medicine and Qi Gong (Chi Kung), which named him the Qi Gong Master of the Year.

The Universal Tao System and Training Center

THE UNIVERSAL TAO SYSTEM

The ultimate goal of Taoist practice is to transcend physical boundaries through the development of the soul and the spirit within the human. That is also the guiding principle behind the Universal Tao, a practical system of self-development that enables individuals to complete the harmonious evolution of their physical, mental, and spiritual bodies. Through a series of ancient Chinese meditative and internal energy exercises, the practitioner learns to increase physical energy, release tension, improve health, practice self-defense, and gain the ability to heal him- or herself and others. In the process of creating a solid foundation of health and well-being in the physical body, the practitioner also creates the basis for developing his or her spiritual potential by learning to tap into the natural energies of the sun, moon, earth, stars, and other environmental forces.

The Universal Tao practices are derived from ancient techniques rooted in the processes of nature. They have been gathered and integrated into a coherent, accessible system for well-being that works directly with the life force, or chi, that flows through the meridian system of the body.

Master Chia has spent years developing and perfecting techniques for teaching these traditional practices to students around the world through ongoing classes, workshops, private instruction, and healing sessions, as well as through books and video and audio products. Further information can be obtained at www.universal-tao.com.

THE UNIVERSAL TAO TRAINING CENTER

The Tao Garden Resort and Training Center in northern Thailand is the home of Master Chia and serves as the worldwide headquarters for Universal Tao activities. This integrated wellness, holistic health, and training center is situated on eighty acres surrounded by the beautiful Himalayan foothills near the historic walled city of Chiang Mai. The serene setting includes flower and herb gardens ideal for meditation, open-air pavilions for practicing Chi Kung, and a health and fitness spa.

The center offers classes year-round, as well as summer and winter retreats. It can accommodate two hundred students, and group leasing can be arranged. For information worldwide on courses, books, products, and other resources, see below.

RESOURCES

Universal Healing Tao Center
274 Moo 7, Laung Nua, Doi Saket, Chiang Mai, 50220, Thailand
Tel: (66)(53) 921-200
E-mail: universaltao@universal-tao.com
Website: www.universal-tao.com

For information on retreats and the health spa, contact:
Tao Garden Health Spa & Resort
E-mail: reservations@tao-garden.com
Website: www.tao-garden.com

Good Chi • Good Heart • Good Intention

# Index

BOOKS OF RELATED INTEREST

The Inner Smile
Increasing Chi through the Cultivation of Joy
by Mantak Chia

Healing Light of the Tao
Foundational Practices to Awaken Chi Energy
by Mantak Chia

Healing Love through the Tao
Cultivating Female Sexual Energy
by Mantak Chia

Basic Practices of the Universal Healing Tao
An Illustrated Guide to Levels 1 through 6
by Mantak Chia and William U. Wei

Chi Self-Massage
The Taoist Way of Rejuvenation
by Mantak Chia

Craniosacral Chi Kung
Integrating Body and Emotion in the Cosmic Flow
by Mantak Chia and Joyce Thom

Iron Shirt Chi Kung
by Mantak Chia

Life Pulse Massage
Taoist Techniques for Enhanced Circulation and Detoxification
by Mantak Chia and Aisha Sieburth

Inner Traditions • Bear & Company
P.O. Box 388
Rochester, VT 05767
1-800-246-8648
www.InnerTraditions.com

Or contact your local bookseller